INVESTIGATE AND UNDERSTAND THE

MIDDLE AGES

BROWN BEAR BOOKS

INVESTIGATE AND UNDERSTAND THE

MIDDLE AGES

Written by Sarah McNeill

Published by Brown Bear Books Ltd
First Floor
9-17 St Albans Place
London N1 0NX

© 2015 Brown Bear Books Ltd

ISBN 978-1-78121-260-8

A catalogue record for this book is available from
the British Library.

Designer: Mary Walsh
Editor: Dawn Titmus
Design manager: Keith Davis
Editorial director: Lindsey Lowe
Children's publisher: Anne O'Daly

Printed in China

All artworks © Brown Bear Books.
Photographs: Shutterstock p.11

Brown Bear Books has made every attempt to contact
the copyright holder. If you have any information please
contact: licensing@brownbearbooks.co.uk

CONTENTS

INTRODUCTION

The Middle Ages lasted for about 1,000 years. Although historians sometimes disagree about dates, it is generally agreed that the Middle Ages began when the last Roman emperor lost power in the West, in 476 CE, and that they ended sometime between 1400 and 1450. We call this period 'medieval'. In many ways, the world built then survives today.

All across Europe there are signs of the medieval past. Many towns and villages were founded in the Middle Ages. Cathedrals show us the stunning artistic and engineering skills people had and their great belief in the Christian God. Castles tell us about the power of the nobles. The landscape was shaped by peasants, who cleared forests so that crops could be grown on the land. Modern political units such as the nations of France, England and Scotland took shape at this time.

FIND OUT MORE

You will be able to find pictures and objects made in the Middle Ages, such as the ones in this book, in museums all over the world.

HOW TO USE THIS BOOK

This book explores and explains the world of the Middle Ages. Each double-page section looks at a particular aspect of life in medieval times, creating a fascinating picture of medieval civilisation.

INTRODUCTION

Concise yet informative, this text introduces the reader to the topics covered in the section. This broad coverage is complemented by more detailed exploration of particular points in the captions.

INSET ARTWORKS

Subjects that help to explain particular points are shown as inset artworks along with an explanation of their significance.

SPOTLIGHTS

A series of illustrations at the bottom of each page encourages the reader to look out for objects from the Middle Ages that can be found in museums.

CASTLES

Castles belonged to kings, no and knights – the most impor people in the land. A castle wa sign that the owner had powe times of both war and peace. C were homes and strongholds at same time. They were designed be difficult for an enemy to atta The first castles were built in th and 10th centuries, from earth a wood. Designs gradually change to suit the new fighting methods

MOTTE AND BAILEY CASTLE
Motte and bailey castles were built in the 11th and 12th centuries. The bailey was an enclosed yard with buildings inside. The motte was a mound of earth with a timber tower on top.

Bailey

LOOK OUT FOR THESE

■ **SPIRAL STAIRCASE**
Spiral staircases were designed to ascend clockwise, so that a right-handed invader, fighting his way in, would hit the stonework if he used his sword.

16

HEADING

The subject matter of each section is identified by a heading clearly displayed in the top left-hand corner.

DETAILED INFORMATION

From the building of magnificent cathedrals to the everyday life of nobles and peasants, a wealth of information helps to build a complete picture of the Middle Ages.

ILLUSTRATIONS

High-quality, full-colour artworks bring the world of the Middle Ages to life. Each section is packed with visual information.

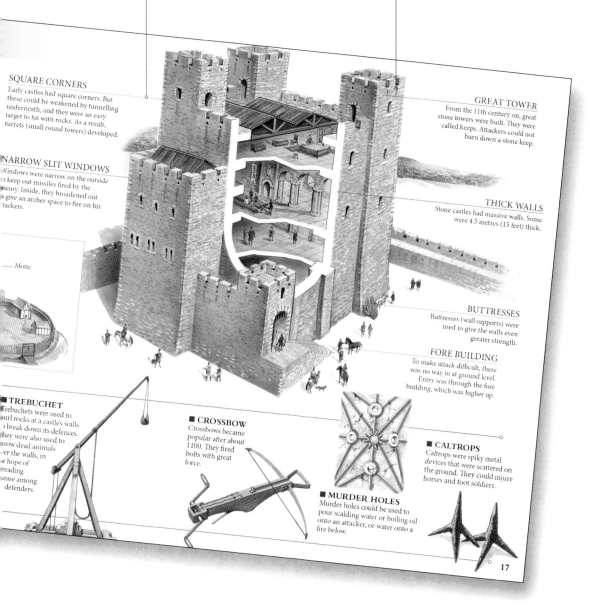

SQUARE CORNERS
Early castles had square corners. But these could be weakened by tunnelling underneath, and they were an easy target to hit with rocks. As a result, turrets (small round towers) developed.

NARROW SLIT WINDOWS
Windows were narrow on the outside to keep out missiles fired by the enemy. Inside, they broadened out to give an archer space to fire on his attackers.

— Motte

GREAT TOWER
From the 11th century on, great stone towers were built. They were called keeps. Attackers could not burn down a stone keep.

THICK WALLS
Stone castles had massive walls. Some were 4.5 metres (15 feet) thick.

BUTTRESSES
Buttresses (wall supports) were used to give the walls even greater strength.

FORE BUILDING
To make attack difficult, there was no way in at ground level. Entry was through the fore building, which was higher up.

■ **TREBUCHET**
Trebuchets were used to hurl rocks at a castle's walls to break down its defences. They were also used to throw dead animals over the walls, in the hope of spreading disease among defenders.

■ **CROSSBOW**
Crossbows became popular after about 1100. They fired bolts with great force.

■ **CALTROPS**
Caltrops were spiky metal devices that were scattered on the ground. They could injure horses and foot soldiers.

■ **MURDER HOLES**
Murder holes could be used to pour scalding water or boiling oil onto an attacker, or water onto a fire below.

17

THE AGE OF INVASIONS

The Middle Ages started with a time of upheaval. The Roman Empire was declining in Western Europe and was invaded by one enemy tribe after another. Vandals invaded Spain and Africa; Jutes, Angles and Saxons invaded England; Goths invaded Italy and France. The Romans called these invaders 'barbarians'. The invaders' way of life was warlike, and their leaders were battle heroes. They set up their own kingdoms, fighting for land and power.

These invasions of the 3rd, 4th and 5th centuries CE were followed by another wave of invasions after about 800. Three new warlike peoples invaded Europe: Vikings in the north, Arabs in the south and Hungarians in the east. Roman civilisation was at an end and a way of life sometimes called feudalism took its place (see pages 10–11).

SHALLOW DRAFT
Viking ships were long and narrow, and had shallow drafts – the depth from the bottom of the hull to the waterline – so they could be sailed far upriver.

LOW SIDES
The low sides of Viking ships allowed the crew to use oars, but usually the ships were sailed.

SHIPWRIGHTS
Vikings were expert shipwrights. They built warships, as well as ships for trading and for fishing. They were the first people in northern Europe to build ships with sails and oars.

LOOK OUT FOR THESE

■ HELMET
Warriors and leaders were buried with their weapons – their most valued possessions. This helmet was found at the site of the Sutton Hoo burial in England.

■ VANDAL MOSAIC
This mosaic shows a Vandal, one of the peoples who invaded the Roman Empire.

■ FOOT SOLDIERS
England was invaded by Angles and Saxons who fought on foot, as this painting shows.

PROW

The prow of a Viking ship would often be carved and decorated. Animal or human heads were popular designs.

WORKING WITH TIMBER

Shipwrights used simple tools, such as axes, saws and adzes. For the intricate carving on the prow, they used chisels, files and gouges.

VIKING SHIPBUILDING

The prow of a Viking ship was carved from a single piece of timber. The hull was built up with overlapping planks.

1. Backbone of the ship (the keel) was laid down first.

2. Overlapping rows of planks were nailed together to form the hull.

3. Cross beams and floor timbers were attached to the hull.

4. Decking and a socket for the mast were added.

■ KING AND COUNCIL

In this Anglo-Saxon painting you can see a king and his advisers. As the invading tribes settled, their leaders became kings, their warriors became nobles and some of the nobles formed a council to advise the king.

■ TREASURE

This gold buckle is part of a treasure buried in the 4th century. War leaders rewarded their followers with rich gifts taken from their enemies. Jewellery, gold, silver and weapons were all very important.

FEUDALISM

'Feudalism' is a word often used to describe the way of life in the Middle Ages. In a feudal country, the king – there were few ruling queens at the time – was not powerful enough to rule by himself, and owning land was important. The king needed supporters all over the country to help him. He gave land to the lords who promised to support him, such as by fighting in his wars. They, in turn, gave some of their land to other people.

Anyone who had received land and promised support was called a vassal. The poor promised to do farmwork or pay rents in exchange for their land.

QUARRELS

When peasants quarrelled with each other, they took their dispute to the lord of the manor's court.

TENANTS

The lord's tenants had to come to his court when he summoned them. They were needed as witnesses in legal cases, as well as for all sorts of other tasks.

LOOK OUT FOR THESE

■ DOMESDAY BOOK

The Domesday Book was a great survey made in England for King William the Conqueror in 1086. It recorded almost all the land in the country and showed that since conquering England in 1066, William had given vast amounts of land to the Normans of northern France.

■ THRONE

A throne was a great sign of authority. Kings, nobles and other important people were allowed to sit, while less important people had to stand.

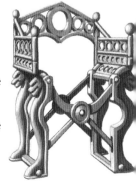

SEISIN

When the lord let a tenant hold land, a special ceremony took place. The tenant was given a clod of earth, which represented the land. This was called 'giving seisin'.

LORD OF THE MANOR

The owner of a manor – an estate in the country – was called the lord of the manor. The lord of the manor had the right to hold a law court for his tenants.

■ CHARLEMAGNE

This bronze statue of the Holy Roman Emperor Charlemagne, who lived from about 742 to 814, is in the Louvre museum in Paris. Charlemagne gave land to his vassals and expected military support in return.

■ THE MAGNA CARTA

In 1215 King John signed the Magna Carta (Great Charter). It said that the king had to follow the laws of the land, and it protected the rights of the nobles against the wishes of the king.

RELIGION

At the start of the Middle Ages, most people believed in paganism. Paganism was the belief that there were gods in natural things, such as the sun and trees. During the Middle Ages, paganism died out and three great religions became dominant instead: Christianity, Judaism (whose followers are called Jews) and Islam (whose followers are called Muslims). Each of these religions teaches that there is only one God. Christianity was the main religion in Europe. Jews from the Holy Land went to many parts of Europe. Islam began in the East in 622. Many wars were fought in the name of religion. The most famous were the Crusades – wars between Muslims and Christians in the Holy Land. These began in 1096 and lasted for 200 years.

ROYAL BELIEVER
If the ruler became Christian, his people did, too.

 LOOK OUT FOR THESE

■ **ICON**
In Eastern Europe, monks made beautiful paintings of Christ and the Virgin Mary, or of the saints, on small wooden panels. These paintings are called icons.

■ **STONE CROSS**
Carved crosses like this one were often set up where the Christian message was first preached by missionaries. A church might later be built nearby.

SACRED OAK
Pagans worshipped gods in the sun, rivers and trees. They believed that spirits inhabited springs and wells.

CHRISTIAN MISSIONARIES
Many missionaries were monks. Christianity was brought to England by a monk named Augustine in 597.

PREACHING THE GOSPEL
Missionaries travelled the country preaching the Christian message from the Bible.

■ JELLING STONES
At Jelling, in Denmark, a 10th-century Danish king set up this elaborately carved stone after he made his people Christian.

■ ISLAMIC PRAYER BEADS
Since the Middle Ages, Muslims have used prayer beads like these to help them to pray.

■ ISLAMIC ART
People created especially beautiful places of worship at this time. Islamic artists produced stunning geometric patterns and were particularly skilled at calligraphy, the art of handwriting.

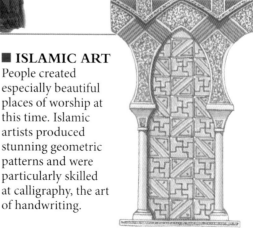

KNIGHTS

Knights were the most important medieval soldiers. Originally, a knight was an attendant. But after about 800, knights in much of Western Europe began to fight on powerful warhorses. Soon fighting on horseback spread to other parts of Europe. Only wealthy men could afford to become knights because warhorses were very expensive. When a man became a knight, he was dubbed, or lightly touched with a sword on the shoulder, by his lord, and given his own sword.

PLATE ARMOUR

Knights wore full suits of armour after about 1400. It was called plate armour and was made of steel.

LADY

Tournaments – competitions between knights – were popular from the 11th century. Many noblewomen came to watch. Some knights swore to serve one special lady.

LOOK OUT FOR THESE

■ SPUR

Warhorses were specially trained to obey their owner's voice, but knights also used spurs like this one to control them. Spurs were worn on the knight's heels. A prick from the spurs urged the horse on.

■ CHAIN MAIL

Knights needed armour for protection. Some of the first armour was made of chain mail. It was made from small iron rings linked together to make a knee-length shirt.

LANCE

The lance was a long pole made of wood. It shattered if it struck a very hard blow.

HERALDRY

A series of designs on knights' shields identified friends and enemies in battle. This is called heraldry.

Fleur-de-lis

Cross

Bend

Gyronny

■ SWORD

The sword was the knight's main weapon. Until about 1250, most swords had a double-edged blade, like this one, and a rounded point. Swords with a pointed end for thrusting came later.

■ RING

A lady might give a knight a ring like this as a sign of her favour.

■ MONUMENTAL BRASS

Knights' graves were often marked by a brass plate like this, engraved with a picture of the knight in armour.

CASTLES

Castles belonged to kings, nobles and knights – the most important people in the land. A castle was a sign that the owner had power in times of both war and peace. Castles were homes and strongholds at the same time. They were designed to be difficult for an enemy to attack. The first castles were built in the 9th and 10th centuries, from earth and wood. Designs gradually changed to suit the new fighting methods.

SQUARE CORNERS

Early castles had square corners. But these could be weakened by tunnelling underneath, and they were an easy target to hit with rocks. As a result, turrets (small round towers) developed.

NARROW SLIT WINDOWS

Windows were narrow on the outside to keep out missiles fired by the enemy. Inside, they broadened out to give an archer space to fire on his attackers.

MOTTE AND BAILEY CASTLE

Motte and bailey castles were built in the 11th and 12th centuries. The bailey was an enclosed yard with buildings inside. The motte was a mound of earth with a timber tower on top.

Motte

Bailey

 LOOK OUT FOR THESE

■ SPIRAL STAIRCASE

Spiral staircases were designed to ascend clockwise, so that a right-handed invader, fighting his way in, would hit the stonework if he used his sword.

■ TREBUCHET

Trebuchets were used to hurl rocks at a castle's walls to break down its defences. They were also used to throw dead animals over the walls, in the hope of spreading disease among the defenders.

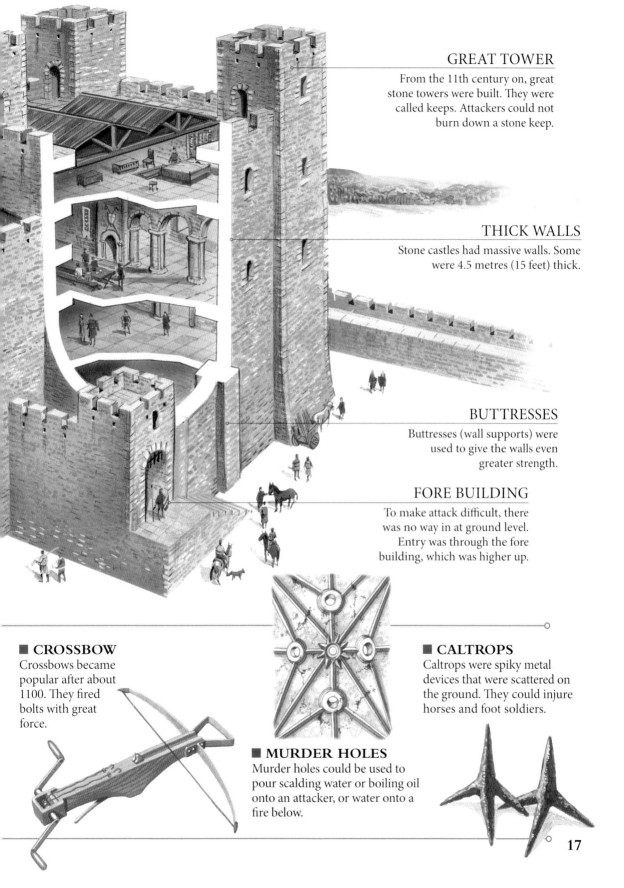

GREAT TOWER

From the 11th century on, great stone towers were built. They were called keeps. Attackers could not burn down a stone keep.

THICK WALLS

Stone castles had massive walls. Some were 4.5 metres (15 feet) thick.

BUTTRESSES

Buttresses (wall supports) were used to give the walls even greater strength.

FORE BUILDING

To make attack difficult, there was no way in at ground level. Entry was through the fore building, which was higher up.

■ CROSSBOW

Crossbows became popular after about 1100. They fired bolts with great force.

■ MURDER HOLES

Murder holes could be used to pour scalding water or boiling oil onto an attacker, or water onto a fire below.

■ CALTROPS

Caltrops were spiky metal devices that were scattered on the ground. They could injure horses and foot soldiers.

WAR

The purpose of a medieval war was to win land, towns and castles from the enemy. Laying siege to castles and towns was an important way of doing this. During a siege, attackers bombarded the walls so that they could enter, or they tried to starve the inhabitants into surrendering. Europeans learned much about siege warfare from the Arabs during the Crusades.

Some wars lasted a long time, such as the Hundred Years' War (1337–1453) between England and France. In this war archers with longbows became important. Wars were supposed to follow a set of rules called the law of chivalry. One rule said that important prisoners were to be ransomed (released after payment) rather than killed. In practice, however, people often ignored the rules.

NORMANS

The Normans were from northern France. They fought on horseback with swords and lances. They were protected by helmets, coats of chain mail and shields shaped like kites.

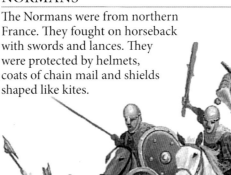

SAXONS

The Saxons were a Germanic tribe. They rode into battle but fought on foot. Their main weapons were spears, maces and battleaxes.

LOOK OUT FOR THESE

■ PENNON

The Bayeux Tapestry tells us much about soldiers and weapons at the time of the Battle of Hastings in 1066. It shows soldiers carrying spears and lances with an oblong flag, or pennon, attached. The pennon indicated high rank.

■ BAGGAGE TRAIN

War was expensive and needed much preparation. The Bayeux Tapestry shows that the Normans had to bring a baggage train of armour, weapons, warhorses and even a castle in kit form with them.

FIGHTING BISHOP

Bishop Odo of Bayeux in Normandy took part in the Battle of Hastings in 1066. He was William the Conqueror's half-brother.

SHIELD WALL

King Harold's bodyguards had been trained to make a wall of shields that would stand up to charges by the Norman cavalry at the Battle of Hastings.

■ LOOTING

Many medieval pictures show soldiers looting their enemies. They made off with armour, weapons like these and even sheep and cattle. In the Hundred Years' War, some soldiers made fortunes this way.

■ STIRRUP

Wearing stirrups helped soldiers keep their balance when fighting on horseback, especially when charging with a lance.

■ MACE

The mace was a weapon used by noblemen. Maces were popular in the 1300s because they could injure an enemy even if he was wearing plate armour.

MONASTIC LIFE

Monks and nuns devoted their lives to God. They lived in single-sex communities called monasteries, taking vows to live in poverty and obedience and not to marry. There were different groups of monks and nuns, such as the Benedictines, Cistercians and Carthusians, but their ways of life were similar. Famous monastery buildings can still be seen at Rievaulx in England and Caen in France, for example.

Monastic life began in Egypt in the 3rd century. It quickly became very popular. Saint Benedict (c. 480–c. 546) set a pattern for monastic life, dividing the days and nights into times for work and times for prayer. Benedict's daily timetable is still used in monasteries today.

GUEST HOUSE
Monasteries had a duty to welcome travellers and to provide them with a bed for the night.

CHURCH
Services and prayers in the monastery church took place day and night.

LOOK OUT FOR THESE

■ TONSURE
Monks had their hair clipped on top. The hairstyle is called a tonsure. This picture shows the English monk Guthlac (673–714) being given a tonsure.

■ MORTAR AND PESTLE
Mortars and pestles were used to pound herbs to make medicines. Monks and nuns were skilled in making herbal remedies.

■ CHALICE
Prayer and worship were the most important parts of life for monks and nuns. At the religious service called Mass they used a special cup, or chalice, like this.

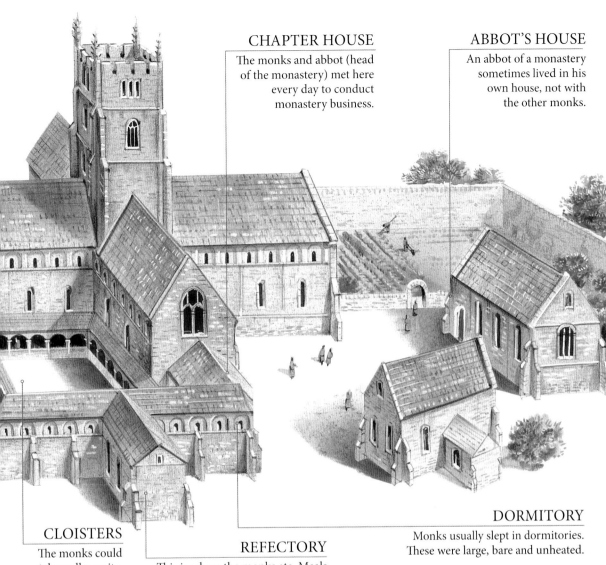

CHAPTER HOUSE
The monks and abbot (head of the monastery) met here every day to conduct monastery business.

ABBOT'S HOUSE
An abbot of a monastery sometimes lived in his own house, not with the other monks.

DORMITORY
Monks usually slept in dormitories. These were large, bare and unheated.

CLOISTERS
The monks could take walks, write, read and pray here.

REFECTORY
This is where the monks ate. Meals were usually eaten in silence.

■ MISERICORD
Misericords were hinged, tip-up seats in the monastery church, often decorated on the underside with carvings like these. Monks and nuns were allowed to lean on the misericords during long services. 'Misericord' means 'mercy'.

■ ROSARY BEADS
Rosary beads were used for prayer. The Franciscan friars – who preached outside the monastery – made the rosary popular.

ART AND ARCHITECTURE

In the Middle Ages, the ability to produce art and architecture was thought of as a practical skill. Artists' work was made to be used, not just admired, as it often is today. Most art and architecture was created for the Church, to help people pray and think about God, or to make the homes of kings and nobles more splendid and comfortable.

For the Church, painters made wall paintings of Bible stories; jewellers and goldsmiths made chalices, shrines and reliquaries (containers for the relics of holy people); sculptors made statues of angels and saints; and architects built churches and cathedrals. For the nobles, artists and craftworkers created tapestries (which were hung on the walls to keep out draughts), tableware, jewellery and highly decorated chests and cupboards.

WORKING WITH STONE

The wheelbarrow was invented in China in the 3rd century and later introduced to Europe. Tread wheels also lifted stone. The wheel turned as a person walked inside it.

BUILDING CATHEDRALS

Building magnificent churches and cathedrals was widely regarded as a way of praising God.

LOOK OUT FOR THESE

■ PAINTED GLASS

Glass windows in glowing colours were made for churches. Some of the finest 12th-century examples can be seen in Chartres Cathedral in France.

■ SCULPTURE

Sculptures in churches were not just there as decorations. They also taught the ordinary people, who could not read, the stories in the Bible. This sculpture shows Jesus appearing to his friends after he rose from the dead.

THINNER WALLS

The Gothic style of architecture became important after about 1150. The biggest difference between Gothic and the earlier Romanesque style was that church walls were much thinner – a result of new building technology.

FLYING BUTTRESS

Flying buttresses support the weight of the building. They were a key feature of Gothic architecture. They allowed walls to be thinner and windows to be larger.

MORTAR

Mortar was made from sand and lime. It was applied to stone with trowels, similar to those used today.

■ MASON'S MARK

Masons put identifying marks on the stones they cut. This was because they were usually paid according to how much work they did.

■ TOOLS

The tools used by masons and sculptors were similar to tools used today: hammers, chisels, axes, saws, squares, punches and gouges.

■ ROMANESQUE

Romanesque buildings, based on the style of ancient Rome, date from the early Middle Ages. Churches built in this period, such as Durham Cathedral in England, have thick walls and huge pillars supporting vaulted roofs.

LEARNING

Few people could read or write in the Middle Ages. Some merchants and tradespeople taught themselves arithmetic and learned to keep their business accounts. The children of noble families learned to read at home. But it was the men, and some women, who served God in the Church – as nuns, priests, monks, friars, bishops and abbots – who were the best-educated people. They learned Latin, which was the language of the Bible, of church services and of many official government documents. Schools were set up in some monasteries and cathedrals, and universities such as those in Paris and Oxford were founded. Here, too, religious studies were considered the most important subjects, but there was growing interest in law and medicine as well.

SCRIPTORIUM

Part of the monastery cloisters was set aside for writing. This area was called the scriptorium.

QUILL PEN

Pens were made from bird feathers. Quills from a goose or swan were best. The pen tip wore down with use and had to be sharpened with a 'pen knife'.

2. Stripped down and tip angled to form a nib

1. Quill from a bird

🔍 LOOK OUT FOR THESE

■ COLOURS

In manuscripts, capital letters were often decorated. Fine beaten gold, called gold leaf, was used. Some colours were made from plant juices.

■ CHARTER AND SEALS

Charters were official documents. They recorded events such as grants of land, the founding of towns and decisions in law cases. A seal proved that the charter was genuine.

ILLUMINATED MANUSCRIPT

Medieval books were decorated with beautiful coloured pictures. They are called 'illuminated manuscripts' because they seem to glow with colour (illuminated) and were written by hand (manuscript).

PARCHMENT

Books and documents were written on material called parchment, which was made from animal skin.

BOOKS

Because books were written by hand – and only a few people could write – they were rare and were treated with great respect. Most books were about religious subjects and were written by monks.

■ LINDISFARNE GOSPELS

This is a page from a gospel book written at the monastery on Lindisfarne, an island off the north-east English coast, about 700. For medieval monks, copying the scriptures was a way of worshipping God.

■ OAK APPLE

Ink, for use with quill pens, could be made from acid and iron galls, a substance found in a growth on oak trees called a gall, or oak apple.

■ STYLUS

Before writers began work, they ruled guidelines for their writing on parchment. They did this by scoring it with a stylus like this one. A stylus had a metal tip and was made from bone.

Peasants

The poorest medieval people were the peasants. They lived in the countryside, where they farmed. The very poorest peasants, called serfs, were not free. They belonged to the lord of the manor and he could sell or give them to someone else if he wanted. They could not educate their sons, marry off their daughters or move away from the place they lived without their lord's permission. They were allowed to grow their own food on a plot of land owned by the lord of the manor. In return, they had to pay rent or work for the lord and farm his fields as well as their own. Farmwork included such tasks as shearing sheep, weeding grain crops, loading hay onto carts, mending tools and collecting honey.

THRESHING

Separating the grain from a crop such as wheat is called threshing. It was the last job of the harvest. A farmworker beat the stalks with a tool called a flail, which separated the grain from the husk and straw.

FOOD

The lord of the manor usually provided food for his peasants at harvest time.

LOOK OUT FOR THESE

■ JOHN BALL

John Ball, seen here in an illustration from a medieval chronicle (record of events), was one of the leaders of a rebellion called the Peasants' Revolt. It started in England in 1381. John Ball wanted freedom and justice for the poor.

■ MANOR HOUSE

The lord of the manor lived in a house like this 14th-century manor house. His peasants provided food for the household. Sometimes they had to give him some of their crops and animals.

OPEN FIELDS

Strips of land belonging to one peasant were scattered in different parts of two or three enormous fields. They were not fenced off from everyone else's.

WOMEN

Peasant women had to toil on the land as well as look after the home and family.

HARVESTING

Cutting the crop was a job the peasants all did together. The lord's crop always had to be cut first.

■ **PLOUGH**

Ploughs turned the soil over to make the fields ready for crops to be sown. They were pulled by a team of eight oxen.

■ **RARE BREED**

People kept many sheep in large parts of England and Spain. Some breeds that were very common in the Middle Ages, like this Leicester Longwool, are rare today but can still be seen on special 'rare breeds' farms.

COUNTRY LIFE

Most medieval people lived in small village communities in the countryside. There were few towns. The local parish church was the centre of village life.

Country life followed a regular pattern every year. In spring peasants ploughed the fields, sowed the crops, and lambed and sheared the sheep. In summer they weeded and manured the crops and made hay. In autumn came the harvest, and in winter wood had to be cut for fuel and many other jobs had to be done.

Each village or manor was more or less self-sufficient (it made or grew everything it needed). There were local craftsmen such as blacksmiths to make scythes, parts for the plough and other farm tools people needed.

THATCHING

A thatcher was a craftsman who thatched roofs. Thatch was made from bundles of reeds.

ANIMALS

Peasants often shared their cottages with their animals. Chickens roosted on the rafters, and there was sometimes a barn for a cow.

LOOK OUT FOR THESE

■ LABOURS OF THE MONTHS

Church carvings often showed peasants doing their monthly tasks. This one shows a man carrying hay in August.

■ FOREST SCENE

Keeping pigs was an important part of village life. In autumn pigs were fattened up, often on acorns and nuts. This picture is from a medieval prayer book. Prayer books often contained scenes of everyday life.

WINDMILL

Each village had its own mill where wheat was ground into flour. Watermills were most common, but windmills came to Europe from the East in about 1150.

COTTAGES

Villagers built their own cottages. Great beams of wood supported the side walls. Windows did not have glass, just wooden shutters to keep out the cold and draughts.

PARISH PRIEST

The priest baptised and sometimes taught village children, buried the dead and performed marriage ceremonies.

STOCKS

People who broke the law were often put in the stocks (wooden boards with holes for the feet) as a punishment. Passers-by could pelt them with sticks, stones and rotten vegetables.

■ SHEPHERDS

This cathedral sculpture shows shepherds and their sheep. Spain was famous for its sheep in the Middle Ages. It had 1 million in 1360.

■ SCYTHE

Sickles and scythes were used for cutting crops. Harvests were smaller than they are today, partly because not much fertiliser was used.

■ PIG STICKING

This prayer book picture of country life shows a pig being killed to provide food for winter – a gruesome but important autumn job. Many animals were killed at this time of year.

TOWNS AND CRAFTS

From the 11th century on, towns grew up in many parts of Europe. Some of these were completely new. Places such as Villeneuve, which means 'new town' in French, date back to this time. Towns were the homes of specialist craftsmen and traders such as grocers, spice merchants, cobblers, apothecaries and goldsmiths. These craftsmen joined together into societies called guilds. The guilds made rules about prices and wages. They had a social side, too. Members met for feasts and for special religious services. In big towns, all the shops of one kind tended to be grouped together. In Florence, Italy, for example, the goldsmiths' shops were all on a bridge called the Ponte Vecchio.

OVERHANGING UPPER STOREYS
Land was expensive, so timber-framed town houses were built so that each storey was wider than the one below, to gain extra floor space.

BUILDING MATERIALS
Most houses were made of wood and plaster. Stone houses were rare and usually built only by wealthy people.

DIRTY STREETS
Shopkeepers threw their waste (scraps, offal, rotten vegetables and other rubbish) out onto the street.

 **LOOK OUT FOR THESE**

■ ITALIAN TOWNS
Italian towns were the wealthiest and most famous of all medieval towns. Townspeople liked to build fine buildings as a sign of their town's greatness. The Leaning Tower of Pisa, in Italy, begun in 1173, was one of these.

■ CHURCH WINDOW
Guilds often paid for church windows – like this one showing a member of the drapers' guild.

■ TOWN WALLS
Towns had walls for protection, as this seal shows. The gates were shut at night so no one could go in or out.

NARROW HOUSE FRONTS

Street frontage was expensive, so town houses and shops tended to be deep and narrow, with the narrow end facing the street.

SHOP SIGNS

Shopkeepers hung out signs that showed people their trade. A tailor hung out a pair of scissors, for example.

APPRENTICES

Children learned trades and crafts by working as apprentices to masters, who were paid to take them on.

■ LOOM

Cloth-making was an important medieval craft. Wool yarn was made into cloth by weavers, who used looms like this one. This type of loom was first used in Europe in about the 13th century.

■ SCALES

Goldsmiths made jewellery, fine tableware and many other precious objects. Their guilds carefully regulated their work by weighing the gold and jewels on scales like these.

TRADE

Fairs were centres for long-distance trade. Merchants from all over Europe and the East gathered to buy and sell their wares. The most famous fairs were held in Champagne, France, every year. There was a 12-day cloth fair, an eight-day leather fair and fairs for other goods, too.

Italy was also an important trading country because of its key position between Europe, Africa and the East. Merchants from Venice traded with the Byzantine Empire through the port of Constantinople (modern Istanbul in Turkey). Merchants from Pisa and Genoa traded with the Muslim cities of North Africa.

As trade increased around the world, so did the development of banks and accounting.

BUYING IN BULK

Large households sent their servants to fairs to buy a whole year's supply of items such as salt or cloth that could not be bought nearer to home.

SHEEP TRADE

Sheep were sometimes driven long distances to market. The Lendit fair, held at Saint Denis in France in June each year, drew shepherds from all over the surrounding countryside.

LOOK OUT FOR THESE

■ SPICES

Spicy food was very popular. Spices such as these cinnamon sticks and cloves were brought to Europe from India and other Eastern countries. The spice trade created great riches for the merchants who bought and sold them.

■ COINS

Coins were made from silver or, more rarely, gold. In Italy there was a gold coin called a florin, and in France one called an *écu*.

■ LAPIS LAZULI

The best shade of blue for painters came from the lapis lazuli stone, shown here as powder in a scallop shell dish. Rare and expensive, the stones came from mines in Central Asia.

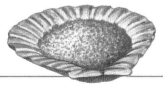

PACK ANIMAL

Goods were carried by pack animals, such as mules, and in carts. Merchants travelled together as protection against robbers.

BANK

Banks grew up to help merchants from different countries pay one another.

MERCHANT

A merchant's aim was to make money. Many people, especially the nobility, thought being a merchant was not a respectable way to live.

■ MERCHANT'S MARK

Merchants had their own mark, or design, to identify the owner of goods sent to fairs and markets. Their mark was often cut into a ring like this. Pressed into melted wax, it could be used as a seal.

■ SILK

Wealthy people wore silk like this. The Italian towns of Florence, Venice and Lucca were silk-weaving centres. Merchants also bought silk called baldachin in Baghdad (in modern Iraq) and cloth called damask in Damascus (in modern Syria).

TRAVEL AND EXPLORATION

Few people travelled far from home. The world beyond Europe was a great mystery, said to contain animals like the mythical centicore – a cross between a horse and a lion, with the voice of a man. But fact began to replace fantasy as travellers and merchants made longer and longer voyages on business.

Marco Polo (1254–1324), a merchant from Venice, was especially famous for his travels. He journeyed as far as the court of Kublai Khan in China. A man who travelled even further than Marco Polo was Ibn Battuta (1304–1369) from Morocco. He visited China and many Muslim countries in South-east Asia and Africa.

SEA FIGHT
Sailors had to defend themselves with weapons if their ship was attacked. They used the same weapons as soldiers on land.

RUDDER
Rudders were invented at the end of the 13th century. They were used for steering.

LOOK OUT FOR THESE

■ ASTROLABE
Sailors used astrolabes to measure the angle of the stars above the horizon as a way of navigating. The best ones were made by Muslims in the East and in Spain.

■ CART
Many medieval pictures show carts like this one. Peasants rode in carts, and prisoners were taken to their execution in them.

■ MAP
This map was drawn in the 1100s. The mapmaker thought the world was a circle divided into four.

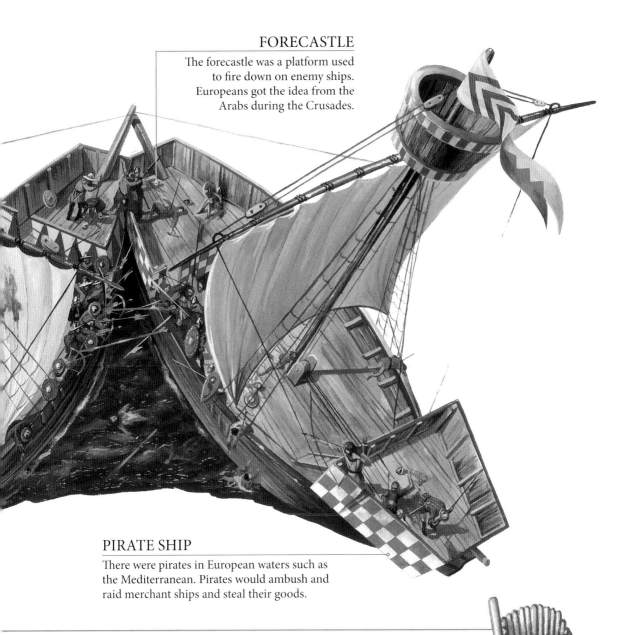

FORECASTLE

The forecastle was a platform used to fire down on enemy ships. Europeans got the idea from the Arabs during the Crusades.

PIRATE SHIP

There were pirates in European waters such as the Mediterranean. Pirates would ambush and raid merchant ships and steal their goods.

■ LITTER

Wealthy women travelled in horse-drawn litters like the one shown in this picture from a medieval manuscript. Nobles travelled more than poor people, visiting their many estates. Their families and servants travelled with them.

■ CREEL

Creels were made from straw or wicker. People carried them on their backs and used them for heavy loads. People in some countries used creels until quite recent times.

ENTERTAINMENT AND HOLY DAYS

Our word 'holiday' comes from the Middle Ages. Then, it meant 'holy day', a special religious feast day when work stopped. There were about 40 to 50 holy days during the year. People were expected to go to three church services each holy day and to fast the night before. But there were plenty of other ways to pass the time. There were entertainers such as jugglers and acrobats. In towns there were processions and plays about Bible stories, such as Noah and the Ark. Some people liked to gamble with dice and to play cards.

PUPPET SHOW

Entertainers such as puppeteers travelled from place to place. They gave performances at castles and manor houses, in villages and at fairs.

LOOK OUT FOR THESE

■ SAINT JAMES OF COMPOSTELA

Many pilgrims prayed at the tomb of Saint James of Compostela in Spain. Pilgrimages were religious occasions, but they were also holidays from work.

■ PILGRIM BADGE

People could buy special badges to show where they had been on pilgrimage and to which saints they were devoted. This badge shows Saint Catherine, who was put to death on a wheel.

TROUBADOUR

Troubadours were wandering musicians. They sang songs, played music and told stories. Especially popular were tales of knights and their ladies, full of heroism and romance.

DANCING BEAR

Some entertainers travelled with performing animals. Bears were trained to dance and apes to do somersaults. Some entertainments were cruel, such as setting dogs to fight bears.

■ BIRD OF PREY

Hunting with birds of prey such as falcons was a well-liked pastime for the nobility.

■ CHESSMAN

Chess was popular with the nobility. Bets were often placed on who would win.

■ HORNPIPE

Music and dancing were favourite pastimes. A typical instrument was the hornpipe – a wooden pipe joined to a cow's horn.

HOMES AND FAMILIES

The father was the head of the family. He made important decisions such as who his children would marry. A nobleman's sons were sent away at about the age of seven to become pages in other noble houses, where they learned obedience and how to use weapons. Girls learned about embroidery, music and how to manage a household. Women had little political power, but there were some exceptions. For example, Joan of Arc led French armies during the Hundred Years' War against England.

PAINTED WALLS
Castle walls were decorated with coloured patterns.

SPINNING
Even in wealthy households, girls learned how to weave and spin so that they could make clothes.

BABY WALKER
Carvings show that some children learned to walk using baby walkers, just as some do today.

LOOK OUT FOR THESE

■ **TAPESTRY**
Tapestries were used as wall coverings in the homes of rich people. This one shows a noblewoman hunting. It was made in Arras, Flanders, in about 1420.

■ **CHEST**
Wooden chests were used for storing linen, clothes, tapestries, jewellery and other goods. They doubled as trunks for carrying belongings when noble families went travelling.

FIRE
Not all rooms were heated, but those that were had roaring log fires.

BATHTUB
A half barrel made a good bathtub. It was filled with warm water from a jug.

RUSH FLOORING
Rushes and herbs were put down as floor covering.

■ **CAPUCHIN**
A capuchin was pulled around the shoulders like a cape and the rest formed a hood. Capuchins were worn until about 1500.

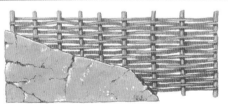

■ **WATTLE AND DAUB**
Wattle and daub was a cheap building material. Wattle was a weave of twigs. Daub was a coating of mud and straw on top.

■ **PRICKET CANDLESTICK**
Pricket candlesticks have a long spike to hold the candle in place. Candles were used to light churches and rich people's homes.

FOOD AND DRINK

Poor people mostly ate vegetables, such as beans and cabbage, coarse bread made from oatmeal or barley, and eggs, cheese and bacon. They drank milk or ale. Rich people had a more varied diet. Hunting provided meat, especially venison (deer meat), for their tables. They ate white bread, drank wine and used spices and rich sauces. Feasts were great social occasions for the rich. The sons of knights served at feasts, carving the meat and pouring water for guests to wash their hands.

Some people wrote books describing good table manners. They advised those eating not to scratch, put their elbows on the table or pick their teeth during meals.

WINE

The best wine came from France and Italy. It was transported and kept in wooden casks, but there was always a risk that it would turn sour when taken long distances.

LOOK OUT FOR THESE

■ FISH

All kinds of fish ended up on the table, from eels to herring. Whale meat was eaten as well. The Church told people to eat fish instead of meat on Fridays, during Lent and at other times in the religious calendar.

■ KNIVES

Knives were valued possessions. Men usually wore one on their belt for use while hunting, as well as for eating. The knives shown here are too elegant for hunting and would have been kept for the table. Forks were used after about 1400.

COOKING ON A SPIT

Meat was roasted on a spit in great households or cut up and boiled in a cauldron. The spit was turned slowly during cooking.

PRESERVING FOOD

There were several ways to preserve food. Fish could be dried, meat salted and hams smoked near the fire.

WASHING

Water had to be brought from a well and carried indoors. Metal cups and dishes were boiled in bran and rubbed with a cloth.

■ AQUAMANILE

Guests washed in scented water brought in beautiful jugs, like this one, called aquamaniles.

■ BEEHIVE

Honey, not sugar, was the usual sweetener, and beehives were a common sight. Hives like this one were made of straw. Wooden bee boxes were also used. Hives and boxes can be seen in many medieval manuscripts.

■ GARDEN PRODUCE

Gardens were not just kept for pleasure. Fruit, vegetables, nuts, herbs and flowers provided food and homemade medicines.

CHANGE AND DISCOVERY

The Middle Ages did not end on one particular day, but after about 1400 ideas began to change, especially about religion. There were also new inventions, such as gunpowder and cannons. These made castles difficult to defend, and knights on horseback ineffective. Deadly plagues hit Europe from 1347, killing at least a third of the people. With fewer people to work the land, the peasants could demand better conditions from their lord. Explorers from Portugal and Spain, such as Bartolomeu Dias (c. 1450–1500) and Christopher Columbus (1451–1506), discovered new lands for Europeans, increasing knowledge of the world. All these changes meant that the medieval, feudal way of life was coming to an end.

BREACH IN THE WALL

Castles no longer made good strongholds once cannons were developed that could severely damage walls and even blow holes in them.

LOOK OUT FOR THESE

■ **PRINTING PRESS**
Johannes Gutenberg invented the printing press in about 1453. Presses like this were soon widely used in Europe. People no longer had to write books by hand.

■ **LIFELIKE ART**
This statue, by the sculptor Verrocchio, is of a great Italian soldier, Bartolomeo Colleoni, who died in 1476. It is an example of the new lifelike style of art that began to develop around 1400.

GUNPOWDER

Gunpowder, which was invented in China, was first used in Europe in about 1250. It was made from sulphur, charcoal and saltpetre. The first weapons to cause explosions did not work very well.

BATTERING RAM

Old ways of fighting, such as using battering rams, continued alongside the new cannons.

CANNON

Cannons of different sizes were used after about 1320. They fired stone (and later metal) balls.

■ CARAVEL

In the 1400s sailors from Spain and Portugal developed the caravel style of ship to withstand rough seas.

■ PLAGUE ATTACK

People feared the pain of plague. They likened it to being shot with arrows, as shown in this woodcut.

■ RELICS

In medieval times people often prayed near saints' relics. This reliquary, or container, held the relics of Saint Faith. But as ideas changed, some relics and reliquaries were destroyed.

TIMELINE OF THE MIDDLE AGES

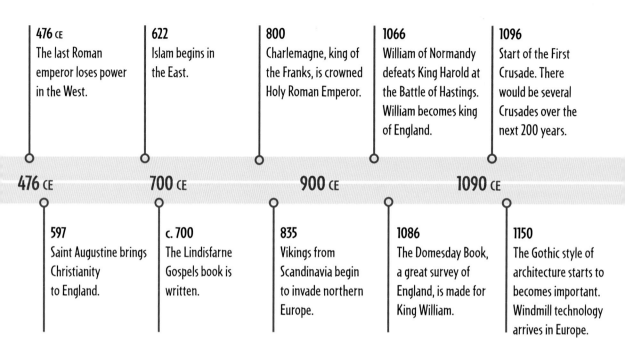

476 CE
The last Roman emperor loses power in the West.

622
Islam begins in the East.

800
Charlemagne, king of the Franks, is crowned Holy Roman Emperor.

1066
William of Normandy defeats King Harold at the Battle of Hastings. William becomes king of England.

1096
Start of the First Crusade. There would be several Crusades over the next 200 years.

476 CE   **700 CE**   **900 CE**   **1090 CE**

597
Saint Augustine brings Christianity to England.

c. 700
The Lindisfarne Gospels book is written.

835
Vikings from Scandinavia begin to invade northern Europe.

1086
The Domesday Book, a great survey of England, is made for King William.

1150
The Gothic style of architecture starts to becomes important. Windmill technology arrives in Europe.

BOOKS

Bingham, Jane, *Medieval World* (Usborne Internet-linked World History), Usborne Publishing, 2012.

Deary, Terry, *Measly Middle Ages* (Horrible Histories), Scholastic, 2007.

Hibbert, Clare, *Terrible Tales of the Middle Ages* (Monstrous Myths), Franklin Watts, 2014.

Jones, Lloyd Rob, *The Middle Ages* (See Inside), Usborne Publishing, 2009.

Macdonald, Fiona, *You Wouldn't Want to Be a Medieval Knight!* (The Danger Zone), Salariya Book Company, 2014.

Medieval Life (DK Eyewitness), Dorling Kindersley, 2011.

Powell, Jillian, *The Middle Ages* (The Gruesome Truth About), Wayland, 2012.

The Middle Ages 1154–1485 (British History), Kingfisher Books, 2007.

Walker, Jane, *Knights & Castles* (100 Facts), Miles Kelly, 2010.

Wheatley, Abigail, *The Middle Ages* (Usborne History of Britain), Usborne Publishing, 2013.

1215
King John of England signs the Magna Carta, a document that says the king is not above the law.

1325
Ibn Battuta sets out on his travels to China, South-east Asia and Africa.

1347–1353
A plague called the Black Death sweeps across Europe.

1415
English King Henry V defeats the French at the Battle of Agincourt.

c. 1453
German inventor Johannes Gutenberg invents the printing press.

1270 CE   **1325** CE   **1400** CE   **1440** CE   **1460** CE

1271
Marco Polo leaves on his journey to explore Asia.

1337–1453
The Hundred Years' War between England and France.

1381
The Peasants' Revolt sees uprisings by peasants in England.

1431
French military leader Joan of Arc is put to death by the English.

1453
The Ottoman Empire captures the city of Constantinople (modern Istanbul), in Turkey.

WEBSITES

www.bbc.co.uk/bitesize/ks3/history/middle_ages/
BBC Key Stage 3 pages about life in the Middle Ages and the diseases, wars and rebellions that made history (archived site).

www.bbc.co.uk/history/british/middle_ages/
BBC History pages on the Middle Ages in Britain, from invasions and the Hundred Years' War, to the Black Death and art and architecture (archived site).

medievaleurope.mrdonn.org/
Mr Donn's pages on various aspects of life in the Middle Ages, such as the nobility and commoners, clothing and food, and the rise of towns.

Note about websites:
The publishers have made every effort to make sure that the websites listed here are suitable for children. However, due to the changing nature of website addresses and their content, we advise that Internet access is supervised by a responsible adult.

GLOSSARY

Words in SMALL CAPITAL letters indicate a cross-reference.

abbey A MONASTERY.

abbot MONK in charge of an ABBEY.

apothecary Someone who mixes and sells medicines, making them out of herbs and other ingredients.

apprentice Boy or girl learning a trade or craft from a master craftworker.

astrolabe Instrument for studying the stars and plotting the course of a ship at sea.

Benedictines MONKS and NUNS who followed the way of life set out by Saint Benedict.

bishop The top church leader in an area. His church is a CATHEDRAL.

Byzantine Empire Part of the Roman Empire that survived in Eastern Europe after the part centred in Rome was conquered. Its capital was Constantinople (modern Istanbul).

Carthusians MONKS who lived a solitary, silent way of life. The order was started in the late 1000s.

castle A stronghold. Also the home of a KNIGHT or NOBLE.

cathedral The most important church in a particular area.

chalice Special cup used at CHRISTIAN religious services.

Christian Someone who believes that Jesus is the son of God.

chronicle Written account of events by someone who lived at the time.

Cistercians Group of MONKS and NUNS – started in the late 1000s – who wanted to live a more simple way of life than the BENEDICTINES.

Crusades Wars fought between CHRISTIANS and MUSLIMS in the HOLY LAND.

draper Someone who sells cloth.

feudalism Society where the people who own land have power over the people who live on it.

friar Man who gave up all his possessions and went out teaching people about God.

goldsmith Craftsman who worked with gold and jewels.

gospel book A book containing the part of the Bible that tells the story of Jesus Christ.

Gothic Style of building used for churches after about 1150.

guild Group of craftworkers or merchants.

Holy Land Parts of the Middle East described in the Bible and the Koran, the holy book of Islam.

illuminated manuscript Text written by hand, with beautifully coloured illustrations.

keep Great stone tower forming part of a CASTLE.

knight Important soldier who fought on horseback.

Latin Language spoken by the Romans. It was still used in the Middle Ages for church services, the Bible and documents.

lord An important person with power over others.

lord of the manor Person who owned a MANOR.

manor Big farm in the country owned by a KNIGHT or NOBLE.

missionary Someone who travels to foreign lands to tell people about God.

monastery Place where MONKS live.

monk Man who takes special religious vows to serve God and lives in a MONASTERY.

Muslim Someone who follows the teaching of the prophet Muhammad and the Islamic religion.

noble Rich and important person.

Normans People from Normandy in France. The Normans conquered England in 1066.

nun Woman who takes special religious vows to serve God and lives in a house with other nuns.

peasant Poor person who lives by farming.

pilgrim Person who goes on a PILGRIMAGE.

pilgrimage A journey to a great church or the SHRINE of a SAINT.

priest Person in charge of a local church, who performs religious services and teaches the local people about God.

relic Something that once belonged to a SAINT. It may be clothes, hair, bones or teeth.

reliquary Special container in which a RELIC is kept.

Romanesque Style of building that was used for churches after about 900.

rosary Prayer beads.

saint An especially holy person, believed by many to be able to work miracles because of his or her faith in God.

Saxons People who lived in England at the time of the NORMAN Conquest.

seisin Occupying a piece of land.

shipwright Person who makes ships.

shrine Holy place where the RELICS of a SAINT are kept.

stocks Wooden construction that held a prisoner's hands or feet. Passers-by would throw things at the person.

tapestry Large, decorative piece of needlework made to hang on the wall of a rich person's house to keep out cold and draughts.

tenant Person who holds and rents a piece of land from another.

tonsure Clipped haircut worn by MONKS.

tournament Mock battle held between KNIGHTS. Tournaments were very popular and crowds flocked to watch.

vassal Someone who swore to be loyal to a more powerful person.

INDEX